Hippopotamuses

by **Judith Jango-Cohen**

mc **Marshall Cavendish**
Benchmark
New York

To my dear sister, Gina Jango Panetta—this is not a comment about your figure

Thanks to Professor Christopher Viney, of the University of California at Merced, for sharing his research
on Bulgy the Hippo, and to Mary Perrotta Rich, who asks the right questions

Series consultant:
James C. Doherty
General Curator, Bronx Zoo, New York

Marshall Cavendish Benchmark
99 White Plains Road
Tarrytown, New York 10591-9001
www.marshallcavendish.us

Library of Congress Cataloging-in-Publication Data
Jango-Cohen, Judith.
Hippopotamuses / by Judith Jango-Cohen.
p. cm.—(Animals, animals)
Summary: "Describes the physical characteristics, behavior, habitat, and endangered status of hippopotamuses"—
Provided by publisher.
Includes bibliographical references.
ISBN-13: 978-0-7614-2238-9
ISBN-10: 0-7614-2238-2
1. Hippopotamus—Juvenile literature. I. Title. II. Series.
QL737.U57J36 2006
599.63'5—dc22 2005026015

Photo research by Joan Meisel

Cover photo: C & M Denis-Huot/Peter Arnold, Inc.

The photographs in this book are used by permission and through the courtesy of:
Animals Animals: 6, Gordon & Cathy Illg; 7, Gerard Lacz; 10, Juergen &
Christine Sohns; 12-13, OSF/Alan Root; 18, Studio Carlo Dani; 31,
Robert Maier; 32, Erwin & Peggy Bauer; 34, ABPL/M. Harvey; 37, Patti
Murray; 39, Norbert Rosing; 40, Manoj Shah; *Judith Jango-Cohen; Peter
Arnold, Inc.:* 4, 14, 20, 25, 30, *C & M Denis-Huot;* 8, 16, Roland
Seitre; 9, 22, Dennis Nigel; 26, A. & J. Visage; 33, S. J. Krasemann;
Photo Researchers, Inc.: 28, Dr. Eckart Pott; 36, Sven-Olof Lindblad.

Editor: Mary Perrotta Rich
Editorial Director: Michelle Bisson
Art Director: Anahid Hamparian
Series Designer: Adam Mietlowski

Printed in Malaysia

1 3 5 6 4 2

Contents

1 Introducing Hippos

A television camera crew paddles down a muddy river in Botswana, searching for wildlife. Up ahead floats a tiny chocolate-colored face with round pink ears and twinkling eyes. With cameras rolling, the crew glides toward the baby hippopotamus. Suddenly the canoe and all twelve passengers rise into the air, then come crashing down. Hidden underwater was a mother Nile hippopotamus. She did not like the boat getting so close to her *calf*.

A Nile hippopotamus is huge. A large *bull* may weigh as much as ten pianos. That's about 8,000 pounds (3,629 kilograms). These giants are extremely powerful because their mass is mostly muscle, not fat.

A young hippopotamus soaks in a pond that fills only during the rainy season.

Even lions and crocodiles steer clear of a hippo's fearsome jaws.

Did You Know . . .

A hippopotamus can rest underwater for four to six minutes. Most people can comfortably hold their breath for less than one minute.

A Nile hippo has monstrous jaws that can open about 4 feet (1.2 meters). A baseball bat could easily prop a hippo's mouth open. In fact, hippos have the largest mouths of any animal except whales.

Scientists have recently realized that *cetaceans* such as whales, dolphins, and por-

6

poises are the animals most closely related to hippos. Both cetaceans and hippos have *red blood cells* that can carry lots of oxygen. This allows a hippo to take a deep breath and stay underwater for long periods of time. Adult hippos can remain comfortably underwater for about five minutes.

Researchers have also discovered that hippos communicate underwater in a similar way to cetaceans. Hippos make clicking and whistling noises, which travel into the water through a roll of fat in the throat. As in cetaceans, dish-shaped areas in the hippo's jaw receive underwater sounds. These sounds then travel to the inner ear.

During the day, common hippos relax together on flat, sandy beaches by shallow streams.

There are two *species*, or kinds, of hippos. The Nile, or common, hippo is the more abundant and better-known type. It lives in the central part of Africa, south of the Sahara Desert. Its *habitat* is waterways near open grassy areas. The pygmy hippo is less familiar to people because it is rarely seen. It lives in the rain forests and swamps of West Africa,

A pygmy hippo's body is pear-shaped; its rump is bigger than its head.

With its mouth closed, a lounging hippo looks harmless.

among tangles of trees and vines. Like the common hippo, it needs to have water nearby.

A pygmy hippo looks different from a common hippo in a few ways. It is much smaller—weighing 350–550 pounds (158–250 kilograms). Compared to its body, its head is not as large. Its legs and neck are longer than the common hippo's. And because the pygmy hippo spends less time in the water, it has developed less webbing between its four toes.

Both species of hippo have the same daily routine, however. They relax or snooze during the day and spend the evening snacking.

Did You Know . . .

A common hippopotamus's wide mouth curves up into its cheeks. When its mouth is closed, it always seems to be grinning.

2 Snoozing and Snacking

A herd of common hippos soaks in a sunny stream. One hippo has a tiny bird perched on its snout. When the hippo yawns, the bird rides up and down, as if on a seesaw. Another hippo pops up from a dive. It exhales as it surfaces, spouting fountains of water from its nose. Then it twirls its ears, sprinkling more water. Special muscles allow a hippopotamus to twist its ears in opposite directions from each other.

A bathing hippo is like an iceberg—most of it is underwater. But a hippo can keep track of what's happening above the water: its eyes, ears, and nostrils are lined up on the top of its head.

Since hippos can't float, these animals are either lying or standing on the riverbed.

Hippos bounce along gracefully underwater.

Birds pecking for bugs in an open wound can hurt a hippo.

14

A hippo cannot float because its body is too dense and muscular. In deep water a hippo closes its nostrils, folds down its ears, and springs along the bottom by pushing off with its back legs, gliding for a bit and then landing with its front legs. Hippos sometimes sleep underwater. Without having to think about it, they surface every few minutes to breathe.

Hippos avoid the heat. Common hippos spend most of their day relaxing and napping in the water. Pygmy hippos shade themselves under trees. The searing African sun is especially dangerous to hippos because they lack the protection of fur. They are nearly hairless, except for their bristly snouts, fuzzy fringed ears, and tasseled tails. Although they have thick skin, the outermost layer is thin, and can crack and lose moisture easily.

A hippopotamus protects itself from the sun by releasing a clear, slimy oil from its skin. The oil, which turns red-orange in the open air, protects hippo skin in four different ways: It blocks the harmful rays of the sun, acting as a natural sunscreen. It prevents

Did You Know . . .

Lots of animals hang out with hippos. Turtles and small crocodiles bask on their backs. Fishing birds use hippos' backs as platforms from which they can scan the area for food. Other birds hop from hippo to hippo picking off ticks and other blood-sucking bugs. Little fishes nibble on deposits caked on hippos' skin. Some even swim around in hippos' mouths, nipping at tidbits stuck between hippos' teeth.

Bacteria in a hippo's stomach break down the plants it eats.

16

hippos' skin from drying out. It kills *bacteria* so cuts heal quickly without becoming infected. And it also appears to repel flies and mosquitoes.

When the sun sets, hippos leave the water and lumber off to their feeding grounds. They always take the same route, scouring deep trails through the brush as they trudge along. Hippos fan out and eat by themselves, except for a mother and calf. Hippos do not need the protection of a herd. Unlike other grazing animals, such as zebras or gazelles, the titanic hippo is rarely attacked by *predators*.

Both species of hippo are *herbivores*. Pygmy hippos use their sturdy teeth to clip leaves, crush hard fruit, and uproot plants. To reach tall tree branches, pygmy hippos balance on their hind legs and lean their front legs against the tree trunk. Common hippos graze on grass. They clip the grass so short that their feeding grounds are sometimes called hippo lawns. Common hippos grab the grass with their thick lips, then rip it off by tossing their heads. They mash their food with their flat back teeth before swallowing it.

Did You Know . . .

The slimy oil released by hippo skin may one day help humans. Christopher Viney, a scientist at the University of California at Merced, spent a year collecting and studying the sticky substance. Professor Viney hopes that his research will lead to the development of a product that combines sunscreen, germ-killing chemicals, and insect repellant. One problem so far: the slime is sort of smelly.

George Washington had a set of false teeth carved from hippopotamus tusks.

Hippos have six front teeth in both their upper and lower jaws. They have four spiked middle teeth flanked by two curved tusks. Males have longer front teeth than females. A bull's lower tusks may be as long as 20 inches (51 centimeters). They are probably longer than your arm. These gigantic tusks are used in defense. But bulls also use them to battle each other for the right to mate with females.

3 Battling Bulls

Two common hippo bulls stand in a river, eyeing each other. They remain on opposite sides of an invisible boundary that divides their territories. Then the bulls turn around, rump to rump. *Splatter! Plip plop!* They swing their tails and bat volleys of *dung* into the water. After completing this task, the bulls stroll back into their territories. The smelly dung serves as a scented message to other bulls that says, "Stay out!"

Common and pygmy hippo bulls defend their territories, keeping out rival males. The bull can then mate with the females that pass through his territory. Pygmy hippo bulls usually live alone. Common hippo bulls set up territories near *nursery* groups of females

This "yawning" bull is not tired but is showing others how tremendous it is.

21

Water erupts from this bull's nostrils as it attempts to frighten a rival.

and their young. Nursery groups usually spread out on sandbars or on flat banks.

The strongest bulls are able to claim territories, or *refuges*, closest to the nursery. Being near the females increases a bull's chances of mating. Young bulls or old, weak ones must settle for refuges that are farther away. As a young bull gets bigger, it challenges other bulls to win a better spot.

A challenge takes place when one bull enters another bull's refuge. Both bulls open their mouths to show off their weapons—their tremendous tusks. They also clamp their jaws together and wrestle to figure out which hippo is stronger. If one of the bulls feels overpowered, it will retreat. Otherwise, a battle begins.

The bulls try to frighten each other. They erupt from the water with a roar, shaking their great heads. They shoot explosions of water from their noses and pelt their rivals with a flood of waves. Each bull swings its open jaws, pounding the other with its piercing tusks. The muddy water soon turns a bloody red.

Bulls do not give up easily. Battles may rage for an hour or more. Eventually, one defeated bull will limp away. He will go off on his own to let his bruised body heal. After he recovers, his skin will carry the battle scars. Sometimes a bull's injuries are so severe that the bull dies. Gashes in its legs may leave it unable to walk, so that it cannot feed itself. Gouges from its rival's tusks may cause it to bleed to death.

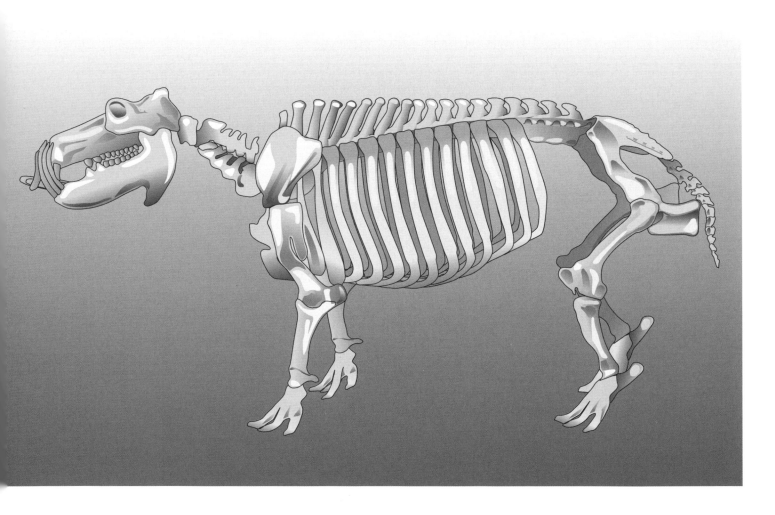

A hippopotamus skeleton has a lot of muscle to support.

The skin of most hippo bulls is etched with battle scars.

The victorious bull takes over the refuge. It will keep its territory as long as it is strong enough to defend it. Its triumph has earned it the right to mate with local females.

If you see two pygmy hippos together, they are most likely a mother and her calf or a mating pair.

Hippos mate in shallow water. After mating, they do not remain together. The bull pairs up with other females who are ready to mate. The female gives birth eight months after mating. She will care for her calf with the help of other *cows* in the nursery.

Did You Know . . .

Pygmy hippos are not as sociable as common hippos. Female pygmy hippos wander the woods alone or with a calf. They do not gather together in nursery groups, as do common hippos.

4 Cows and Calves

A hippo herd yawns and naps on a sunny beach. Farther downstream, behind a curtain of leafy branches, a female lies in a quiet pool. The cow has come here to be alone. Then, with a *plop*, a tiny head appears at the top of the water. It is a newborn calf. The baby has *instinctively* paddled to the surface to take its first breath of air. Being born in the water helps protect it from predators such as leopards, lions, and hyenas.

Hippopotamus calves are usually born in the rainy season. Grasses grow long and lush during this time, so there is plenty for the hippos to eat. They take advantage of the rainy season's bounty to grow strong and gain weight. They will have less to eat during the dry season.

Hippo herds may range in number from ten to more than one hundred.

Hippo mothers are about ten years old when they give birth to their first calf.

Cows with calves must fill up on extra food so they can produce milk for their young. Hippos are *mammals*, so the calf's first food is its mother's milk. Shortly after it is born, a calf searches for its mother's milk. It nudges around her body until it finds the teats near her hind legs. Sometimes a calf nurses underwater. It pokes its nose into the air every thirty seconds for a breath.

A mother hippo keeps her baby away from the herd for a few weeks. During this quiet time, the cow and calf bond with each other. The baby snuggles its tiny head against its mother's snout. They lick and nuzzle each other. The cow gently scratches the calf's skin with her tusks. Sometimes the calf climbs onto its mother's back for a nap.

If her calf strays away from her, the mother may teach it a lesson by nipping the calf or toppling it with a toss of her head. A cow must keep her calf close to protect it from predators. In the water, she guards her baby from circling crocodiles. Poking her head below the surface, she checks for the silent approach of this clever hunter. On land, the hippo mother watches for lurking lions or hungry hyenas.

A young male usually stays with its mother until it is four or five years old.

After a few weeks the mother leads her calf to the nursery. She senses that the calf has learned enough and is strong enough to follow her. At first, she only allows young hippos near her baby. She keeps bigger hippos away with a growl. In the nursery, the baby plays with one another calves. The young hippos splash and tumble over one another. They hook their jaws together in tug-of-war games.

All the cows in the nursery take turns looking after the young calves. Until calves are about four months old, they stay behind while their mothers walk to the

Young hippos play "gaping" games by wrestling with their open mouths.

At about seven weeks old, calves become frisky and start exploring.

feeding grounds. Cows protect the babies from predators as well as from rowdy bulls that enter the nursery. If a bull gets too rough, the cows band together and chase him off.

Although a female calf remains in the nursery when she grows older, a young male must move out to claim a refuge. He may even have to wander off to another herd to find one. For the rest of his life, the bull will have to hold and guard his refuge.

**Did
You Know . . .**
Hippos seem to like to play! One researcher observed a bull playing water games with a baby hippo. The calf kept climbing into its father's mouth. Each time, the bull tossed the baby into the water.

5 Hippos and Humans

A tour guide steers his motorboat to shore and stops the whirring engine. As his passengers hop onto the beach, the guide glances over his shoulder. Charging toward them with wide-open jaws is a hippo bull. The tourists scramble back into the boat and the guide tugs the cord to start the motor. As the boat roars to life, the bull's slashing tusks get closer and closer. He tears after the boat, which rips away from the shore. Skipping over the water, the little motorboat leaves the big bull behind.

Wandering into hippopotamus territory can be a deadly mistake. Bulls defend their refuges against any intruder. Cows can be as ferocious as bulls if anyone comes between them and their calves. A hippo may

This bull's stare seems to say, "Don't come any closer!"

35

When waterways are dammed, causing rivers to dry up, hippos must find other water sources to survive.

also charge a person who is blocking its pathway to the water. This is because hippos seek the safety of water when threatened. If their route to the water is cut off, they become frightened and may attack in panic.

Problems also occur when hippos enter human territory. Both humans and hippos need to live in areas near water. As the human population of Africa increases, people and hippos are living closer together

Scientists warn that more of the hippos' habitat must be safeguarded if the hippo is to survive.

and the area is becoming more crowded. Hippos roam into farmers' fields, trampling or devouring crops. Some angry farmers shoot the invading hippos.

People shoot hippos for other reasons, too. Some hunt hippos for their meat. Others kill hippos to collect their long ivory tusks. These tusks can be carved into expensive objects. Since the selling of elephant tusks was banned in 1990, more hunters are targeting hippos.

One of the most serious threats to hippos is the destruction of their habitat. As the human population grows and takes over more territory, hippopotamus habitat shrinks. Crops are being planted where hippos once grazed, and forests, where pygmy hippos live, are being cut down for timber and cleared for villages. Waterways are being dammed to irrigate farmland. This leaves hippos without enough water, especially in the dry season.

Fortunately, most wild Nile hippos live in protected areas, such as national parks and wildlife sanctuaries, where hunting is not permitted. People are allowed in, however, to observe and photograph the intriguing animals. Protected places are necessary for hippos to survive. The World *Conservation* Union reports that the populations of both hippo species are declining. A 2004 survey found that there are fewer than 150,000 wild common hippos and only between 2,000 and 3,000 wild pygmy hippos.

The movement of hippo herds keeps waterways clear of clogging plants, helping many animals to survive.

Tourists pay thousands of dollars for tours to see wild hippos.

When the number of hippos in an area drops, farmers suffer. Why? When hippos return to the water after a night of feeding, they lounge around digesting their food. An adult hippo may have eaten 100 pounds (45 kilograms) of grass, which eventually becomes dung, a natural fertilizer. Without this nutrient-rich water, farmers' crops do not grow well.

Fishers discover that as the number of hippos declines, their catch becomes worse. What could hippos have to do with fish? Tiny plants grow in the fertilized water. The plants feed fish, which then feed larger animals such as birds and crocodiles. African waterways without hippos may become nearly lifeless.

Most of us will never have the chance to travel to Africa to watch a wild hippopotamus, with its whale-sized jaws and teddy bear ears. But isn't it wonderful to know that this fantastic and curious-looking creature still exists.

Glossary

bacteria: Microscopic living things, some of which cause disease.

bull: A grown male hippopotamus.

calf: A young hippopotamus.

cetacean: The group of marine mammals that includes whales, dolphins, and porpoises.

conservation: The protection of living things and their natural environment.

cow: A grown female hippopotamus.

dung: Animal waste; manure.

habitat: The natural surroundings or environment where an animal lives.

herbivore: An animal that feeds only on plants.

instinctively: Acting with inborn knowledge.

mammal: A warm-blooded animal with a backbone that has fur or hair, gives birth to live young, and makes milk to feed its young.

nursery: Female hippos and their young.

predator: An animal that hunts and eats other animals.

red blood cells: Cells that pick up oxygen and carry it to other cells in the body.

refuge: The territory that an adult male defends as its own.

species: A particular type of living thing.

Find Out More

Books

Arnold, Caroline. *Hippo*. New York: Morrow Junior Books, 1989.

Brust, Beth Wagner. *Hippos*. Poway, CA: Wildlife Education, Ltd., 2000.

Cole, Melissa. *Hippos*. Farmington Hills, MI: Blackbirch Press, 2002.

Encyclopedia of Mammals, Vol. 7. Tarrytown, NY: Marshall Cavendish Corporation, 1997.

Markert, Jenny. *Hippos*. Chanhassen, MI: The Child's World, Inc., 2001.

Schlein, Miriam. *Hippos*. New York: Aladdin Books, 1989.

Stewart, Melissa. *Hippopotamuses*. New York: Children's Press, 2002.

Trevisick, Charles. *Hippos*. Milwaukee, WI: Raintree Children's Books, 1980.

Walker, Sally. *Hippos*. Minneapolis: Carolrhoda Books, Inc., 1998.

Web Sites

Creature World: Hippopotamus
www.pbs.org/kratts/world/africa/hippo/

Hippopotamus
www.whozoo.org/Intro98/herrick/sethherr.
htm#physical

Hippopotamus
www.yptenc.org.uk/docs/factsheets/animal_facts/
hippopotamus.html

IUCN Hippo Specialist Subgroup: Just for Kids
moray.ml.duke.edu/projects/hippos/
JustForKids/JustKidsHome.html

Nile Hippopotamus
nationalzoo.si.edu/Animals/AfricanSavanna/
fact-hippo.cfm

Pygmy Hippopotamus
nationalzoo.si.edu/Animals/AsianElephants/
factpygmyhippo.cfm

Index

Page numbers for illustrations are in **boldface**.

About the Author

Judith Jango-Cohen's intimate knowledge of nature comes from years of observing and photographing plants and wildlife in forests, deserts, canyons, and along seacoasts. Titles from her forty children's books have been recommended by the National Science Teachers' Association, chosen for the Children's Literature Choice List, and named a Best Children's Book of the Year by the Children's Book Committee at Bank Street College. You can find out more about her books and school visits at www.jangocohen.com